HAPPY HELPERS

Pattern Book

The Art of Creating Cooperation at Home

By Suzanne Hansen
Illustrated by Kathy Pitt

Copyright © 1998 by Suzanne Hansen and Kathy Pitt
All Rights Reserved
Printed in the United States of America
First Printing: August 1998

98 99 01 02 03 04   10 9 8 7 6 5 4 3 2 1

Happy Helpers Pattern Book
Covenant Communications, Inc.
ISBN 1-57734-308-5

Contents

Introduction

Loving to work never came naturally to me as a child, and cooperation was even more difficult to master. Only later in my life, when I started to receive the *benefits* of my cooperation and labor, did I begin to look forward to tasks with anticipation rather than dread.

Then I became a wife and the mother of three very lively children, and I started to get behind. There was more to do at home than one person could handle. My husband, Michael, helped when he was available, but my young children could undo in minutes everything that took us hours to accomplish. It was exasperating. I needed not only my children's help, but their *cooperative and willing attitudes* as well.

The Case for Cooperation

If you've tried the "dictator" approach and other techniques to get your children to help, I'm sure you've come to the same conclusion I did: The only real and lasting key to getting the kids to help happily is to win and keep their cooperation. Granted, they need to share the responsibilities of home life; but they also need to be motivated to do it. Learning to willingly accept these small duties now will better prepare them to meet the larger responsibilities that life will soon place on their shoulders.

The Action Method

Admittedly, it's hard to help your five-year-old understand the idea of cheerful cooperation when she *doesn't like* to make her bed, or your ten-year-old *would rather play* with her friends, or your eight-year-old keeps saying that *he can't*. Rather than stay discouraged, I tried the action method—I did something about it. The results are in this book and in *pattern form*, so you can duplicate my success in your own home and know the joy of increased cooperation. You'll also save a lot of time and headaches in the process.

A Place to Start

The job charts you make from the patterns are by no means a complete answer to creating cooperation in your home; but they are a start, and they will make an immediate difference. A job chart or list of duties serves as the starting point—the *initial road map that guides your children through the tasks you expect them to do.* The charts in this book are designed to make their "task trip" not only fun, but motivating—especially when you use the *awards and badges* that are part of the patterns.

One a Month

You'll notice there are twelve job chart patterns in this book. The reason is basic: variety is the spice of life. Be sure to change the job chart regularly, at least monthly, even if one is working very well. (You can always go back to it in six months.) This will keep things fresh and exciting, and cooperation will be enhanced.

Yes, it will take work on your part. But believe me, the effort pays off in the willingness of your children to help you and in the good work habits they'll start to form. Even if your children are good helpers now, the use of these charts will only make your home life more organized—and more FUN!

Getting Started

Get Your Own KMK (Kid Motivational Kit)

The best way to start anything is to take it one step at a time. After obtaining this pattern book, your next step is to gather together what I call the *Kid Motivational Kit*, or the KMK.

The basic KMK is made up of two or three sheets of poster board, a new package of multi-colored markers (these belong *only* to Mom or Dad), a bottle of glue, scissors, a roll of wide masking tape, and a package of colored construction paper. Get a nice, big, sturdy box to put these things in, and find a safe place for your poster board.

Now that you have the basics, you are ready to personalize your KMK. I like to collect "kiddie stickers." There are all kinds of different stickers—from smiles to flowers, animals to cartoon figures, etc. (I even found some little pickle stickers once that were the inspiration for my *You're a Dilly of a Worker* chart.) I use all these fun stickers to measure progress, spotlight accomplishments, and add color to the charts. The kids really love them, too.

Save household odds and ends for your kit. Cut colorful drawings out of magazines and save cereal box illustrations to help decorate your charts. Use leftover Christmas bows and ribbon to add even more color. I find it's easy to be more creative when I have supplies at my fingertips.

Lack of Money Should Never Stop You!

And by the way, *lack of money should never stop you!* Use the kids' crayons to color your patterns until you get markers. If you can't afford poster board, tape the colored patterns to your refrigerator door and write out your individual children's jobs on separate pieces of paper. Until you get stickers, use a pencil to make simple check marks next to completed tasks. JUST GET STARTED. We do have the power within us to change our circumstances, but we must first believe and then act. So get ready, get set, DO IT!

How to Use the Patterns

To make the job charts work for you, keep in mind the following important elements.

1. Follow the Instructions

The instructions will give you ideas on how to use each chart. They will also help you develop themes around the charts and make them more than just task lists and cute pictures. Each one will become an exciting and motivational event in your home.

2. The Patterns

These beautiful illustrations can be used either as the actual job charts or copied and enlarged for in-home use. Simply color them, cut them out, arrange them on a half sheet of poster board, glue them down, and then write down the tasks your children are to complete. Now, watch your children enthusiastically do their assignments as busy bees, sunshine helpers, minute minders, helpers who give a hoot, etc.

3. Badges and Awards

Included with the patterns are delightful little awards you give your special helpers, and badges for them to wear that brag about their good deeds. Use these frequently and with great fanfare and enthusiasm. No doubt about it . . . it's a lot easier for children to cooperate with parents who recognize their achievements.

4. It's Fun Being Positive

No chart alone will be able to turn a miserable home into a happy, cooperative one. Unhappy behavior and bad work habits are not changed as easily as the spell was broken for Sleeping Beauty. However, change will surely come as unhappy, discouraged attitudes are exchanged for happy, enthusiastic ones. Also, you and your children will see for yourselves that it's *fun* to be positive, busy, and productive.

5. Save Those Charts!

One last word. It's important that you don't waste your efforts. Your charts can easily be stored under a bed or in a closet. Then, when you don't have enough time to make a new one, simply take out an old favorite and relive the good times. This is a wonderful way to keep enthusiasm high and save time and duplication of effort, too!

Pattern #1

Busy Bees

When I first started using job charts, they were simple lists of tasks that were checked off when each job was completed. The first really imaginative job chart I made was a real hit. The pattern for it is entitled simply *Busy Bees*. I got the idea one morning when I was going through some of my craft supplies and noticed a package of little cartoon bumble bee stickers I had purchased some time before. The words *Busy Bees* popped into my head, and I was off.

Making It Work For You

First, color the lettering in the pattern a bright color: "I'm A Busy Bee All Day . . . At Work Or Play!" Then color the little bees. This is where you can get the kids involved. Next, paste the lettering and the little bees on a half sheet of poster board, and using a black marker, write down your children's jobs. If they have several individual responsibilities, make up their lists on separate sheets of paper and place them on the fridge or on the wall under the *Busy Bee* headline you colored and cut out.

Sweet Treats For Busy Bees

Next, color the big beehive, mount it on a piece of poster board, cover it with individual sticks of gum or other sweet treats, and label it *Sweet Treats for Busy Bees*. This will be their reward for doing all their tasks for three days, a week, or any time period you feel will keep them motivated.

How do you keep track of when they complete their tasks? They can either put their initials by each job completed each day, or attach a little sticker when they have completed all their work. Simply count the stickers or initials, and you'll know exactly when they've earned their sweet treat.

Badges and Awards

Keep the enthusiasm going by coloring, cutting out, and pinning the bee badges on your little ones when they do especially well. Make a big deal out of it! They'll be thrilled, and you'll reinforce the idea that *being busy is good.*

When you're either halfway through or at the end of the period of time you are using the *Busy Bee* chart, prepare a special *awards banquet.* Put out the fine china, prepare an extra good meal, and after dessert, have the *Happy Hive Awards* and *Buzzy Bee Awards.* This is where Dad gets into the act. He invites each child to come forward, and the rest of the family gives the child a standing ovation. Then Dad ceremoniously presents the award to the child and tells why that child has earned it. Through all the smiles and fun, the spirit of cooperation and enthusiasm will rise to a higher level in your home. The children will hardly be able to wait to see which chart and ideas you'll unveil next!

I'm a Busy
all day... at
work or play!

I'M A BUSY BEE
ALL DAY
WHETHER I'M
AT WORK OR PLAY!

1. MAKE BED
2. GET DRESSED
3. WASH FACE
4. COMB HAIR
5. TIDY ROOM
6. SET TABLE
7. TAKE OUT GARBAGE
8. PRACTICE PIANO

AFTER DINNER-
1- CLEAR TABLE
2- HELP TIDY UP
3- PREPARE
    FOR BED
4- STUDY/STORY-
    TIME

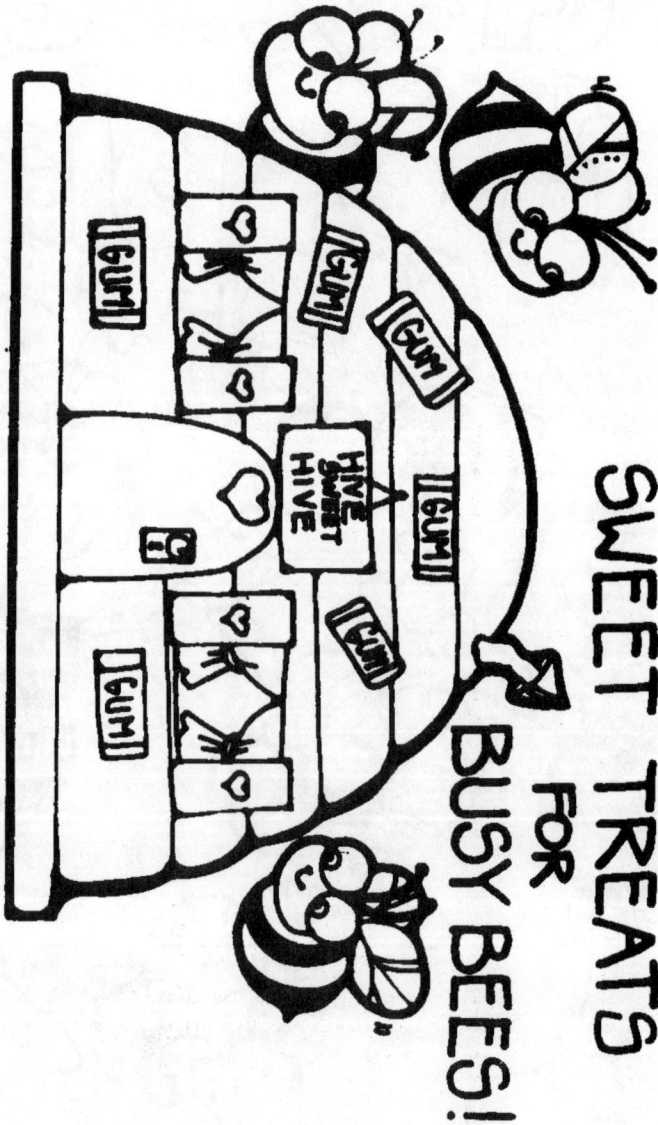

SWEET TREATS FOR BUSY BEES!

GUM

GUM

GUM

GUM

GUM

GUM

HIVE SWEET HIVE

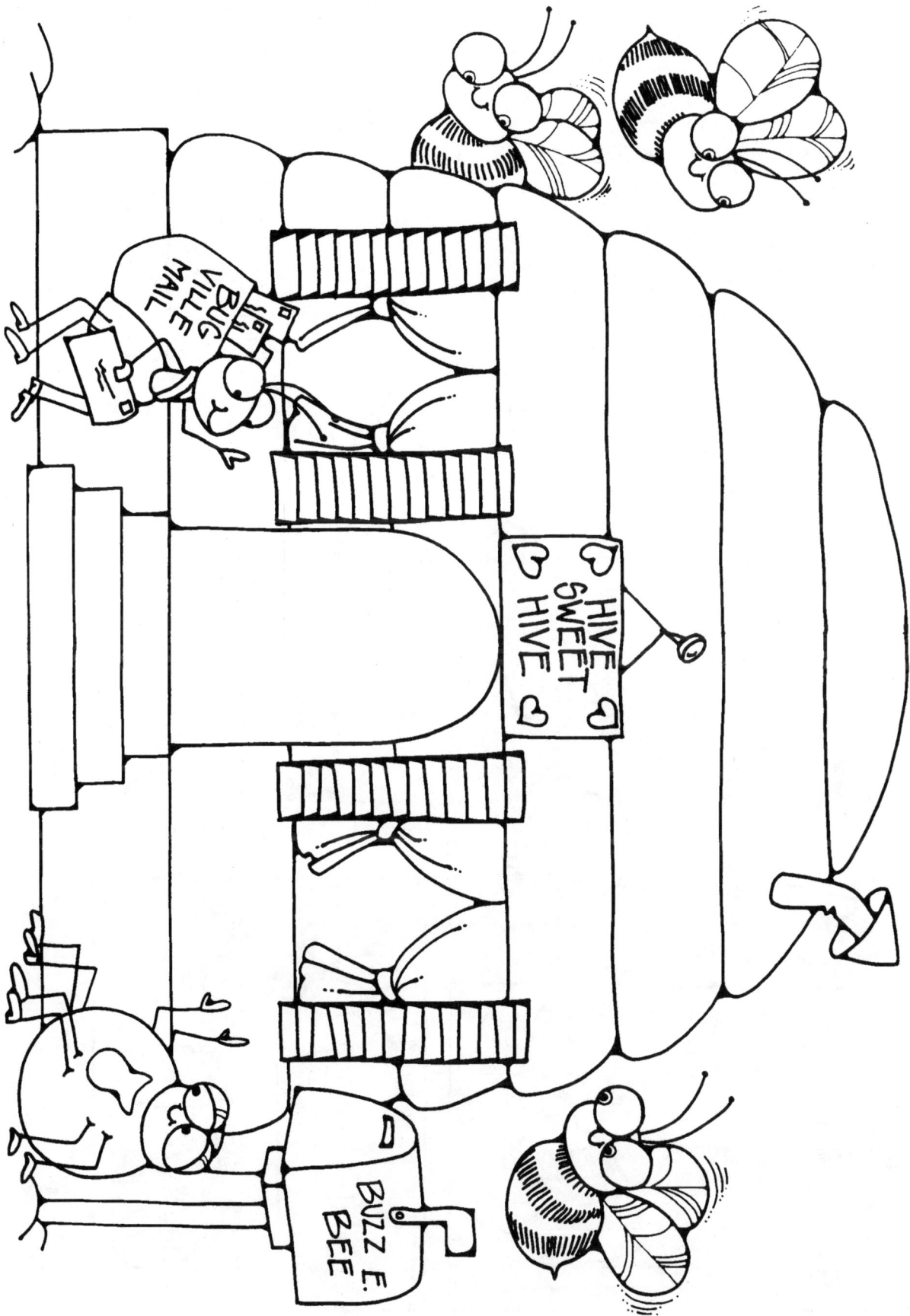

OUR BUZZY BEE AWARD

AWARDED TO:

_____
for work over and
BEE-yond the BUZZ
of duty!

signed _____

HAPPY HIVE AWARD

PRESENTED TO:

For happily
helping around
the hive!

BUZZ!

signed _____

OH SWEET BEE THANKS FOR HELPING ME!

♥HONEY DO HELPER

HAPPIER HIVES Are When Bees Are HUMMING and HELPING HAPPILY!

FOR THANKS FOR BEE-ING YOUR BEST

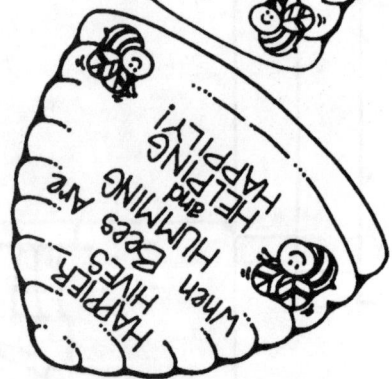

HAPPIER HIVES When Bees Are HUMMING and HELPING HAPPILY!

HAPPY HIVE AWARD

PRESENTED TO:

For happily
helping around
the hive!

BUZZ!

signed _____

OUR BUZZY BEE AWARD

AWARDED TO:

_____
for work over and
BEE-yond the Buzz
of duty!

signed _____

6

Pattern #2

Super Sunbeam

Super Sunbeam is not a job chart. It is a theme pattern to be used for a week or two in conjunction with a simple task list. The main focus of *Super Sunbeam* is to create a better atmosphere in the home, one that will enhance cooperation and motivate each family member to try to be a *ray of sunshine.*

Our family has a lot of fun with this one. The actual inspiration for it came from the song, *You Are My Sunshine.* To utilize this theme, do the following:

1. ***The Big Sun.*** Cut out the pattern of the big sun after coloring it. Put it in the place in your home where you keep the job charts. Then color and cut out the little suns, placing them all around the house to serve as reminders of your new theme.

2. ***The Job List.*** Under the big sun, place a simple job list of everyone's individual responsibilities written on a sheet of paper.

3. ***The Name Poster.*** Next, on a half sheet of poster board, write each child's name down the side, leaving space in between each name. Each day, each child collects sunbeams (sunshine or smiling stickers) and sticks them on the poster by their name. They earn stickers by *first* getting their jobs done *cheerfully,* and then by being kind, showing love, or giving service. It was both fun and interesting for me to have my kids tell me each time they did a kind deed.

4. ***Set A Sunshine Goal.*** I highly recommend that you do this with your children. It really worked well for us. The children picked a certain total of sunbeams they would earn by the end of each week. We wrote this total by each of their names so they could see how they were doing. It was a very high number, so they had to work at it. This theme has made a big difference in our home.

5. *Today's Super Sunbeam.* Start with the pattern, color the sun, mount it on about a quarter sheet of poster board, and cover it with transparent contact film. There's a place on this pattern for a child's name and the date. On the *Awarded Because* lines, write in grease pencil (it comes off easily) why a certain child deserves to be recognized. Then at dinnertime, when all are present, hold up the chart and honor the individual. Spend plenty of time emphasizing what he or she did, then give the child a warm round of applause and a hug.

6. *Sundrops For Sunbeams.* As an added incentive, I converted a mayonnaise jar into a *Sunbeam Jar* by taking off the label and gluing colorful paper or fabric to the lid. Then on the front of the jar I taped a new label (use one of the small sun patterns) that read *Sundrops for Sunbeams.* When the children received five sunbeam stickers, they received a sundrop. The child honored as *Today's Super Sunbeam* got a few extra. What are sundrops? I used lemon drops. Anything will do, but lemon drops are sunshiny and readily available.

7. *Decorate.* I really enjoyed this Sunshine theme. I draped yellow crepe paper all around the kitchen and put little paper sunshines all over the house. I even tried extra hard, personally, to keep a sunny disposition. I also reminded my children of the desired behavior by frequently asking, "Who's going to be our Super Sunbeam today?"

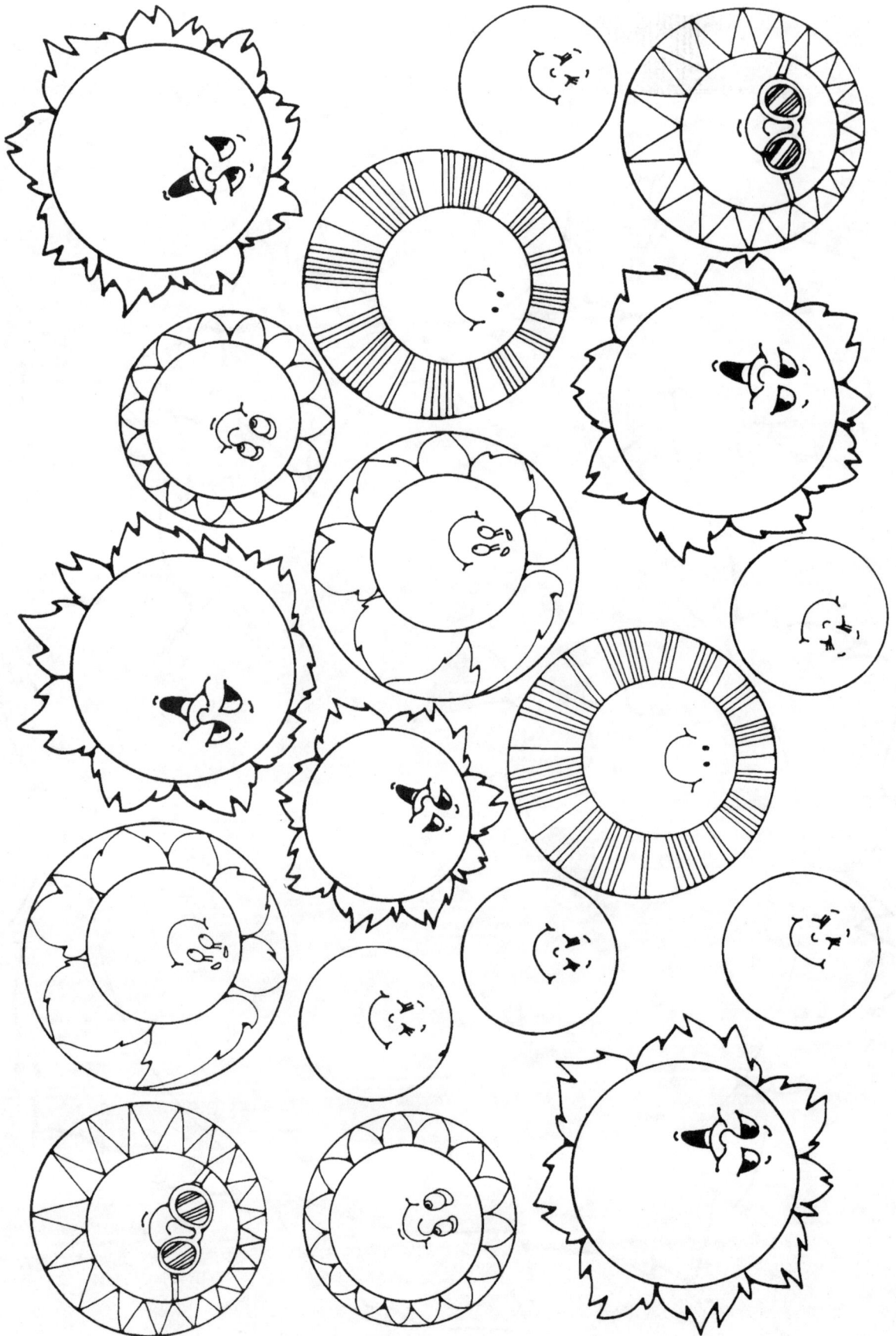

Today's Super Sunbeam

Name _____

Date _____

Awarded Because:

_____

_____

_____

SUNDROPS FOR SUNBEAMS

Pattern #3

Caring Carrot Family

Young children love this chart. They get to pluck out of the ground a colorful, smiling carrot that has one of their jobs written on it. They hurry and do the task, then pluck another.

If your children are very young and can't read the jobs you write for them on the carrots, just draw simple pictures that they can associate with the job. Or you may use the small job symbols included with the patterns. For example, a bed means *make bed;* a toothbrush means *brush teeth;* a dish means *take your dishes to the sink;* a toy means *pick up toys,* etc. By using drawings or the symbol patterns, even three-year-olds can learn to help.

The Patterns And Award

To make the job chart, start with a half sheet of poster board. Next, cut out of brown construction paper a piece about 12 to 15 inches long by five inches wide. Tape or glue this onto the bottom of the poster board, forming a pocket that is open at the top. This becomes the "ground" from which the carrots are plucked. Next, color the sun and the title, *Caring Carrot Family,* and glue onto the chart. Finally, color the carrots, write or illustrate the jobs on them, and you are ready to go. The big picture of the Carrot Family is for the fridge or any place that is easily seen by the family. Color it, and it's ready to go.

The badges and award enclosed with the patterns will round out this cute little chart and will help increase caring through cooperation in your family.

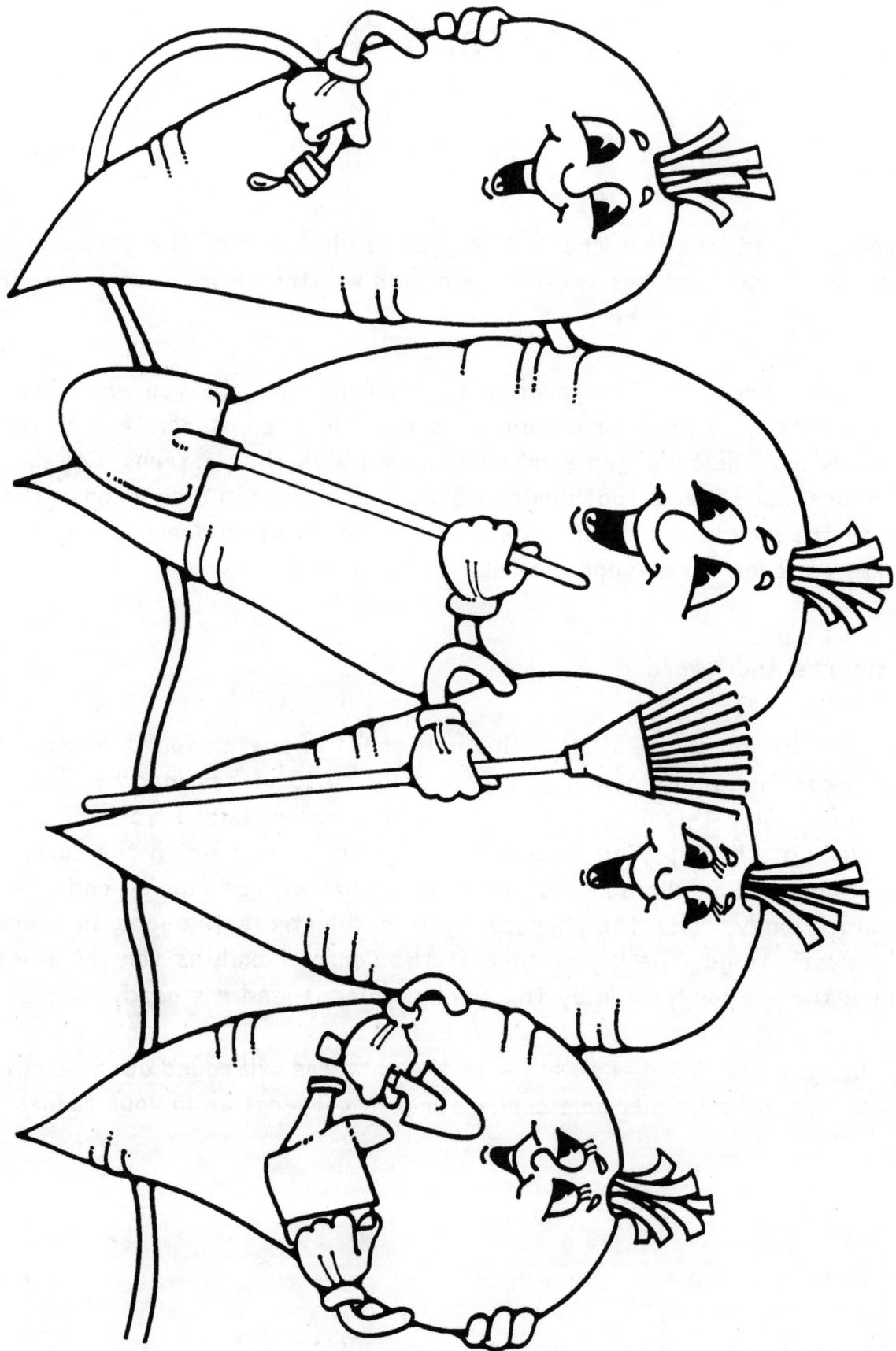

The root
of our
home
is
LOVE!

Caring Carrot
Family

I SHOW I CARE WHEN I MAKE MY BED

Caring Carrot Family

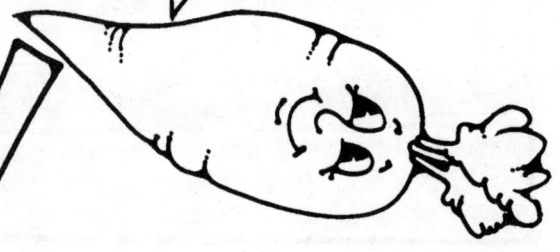

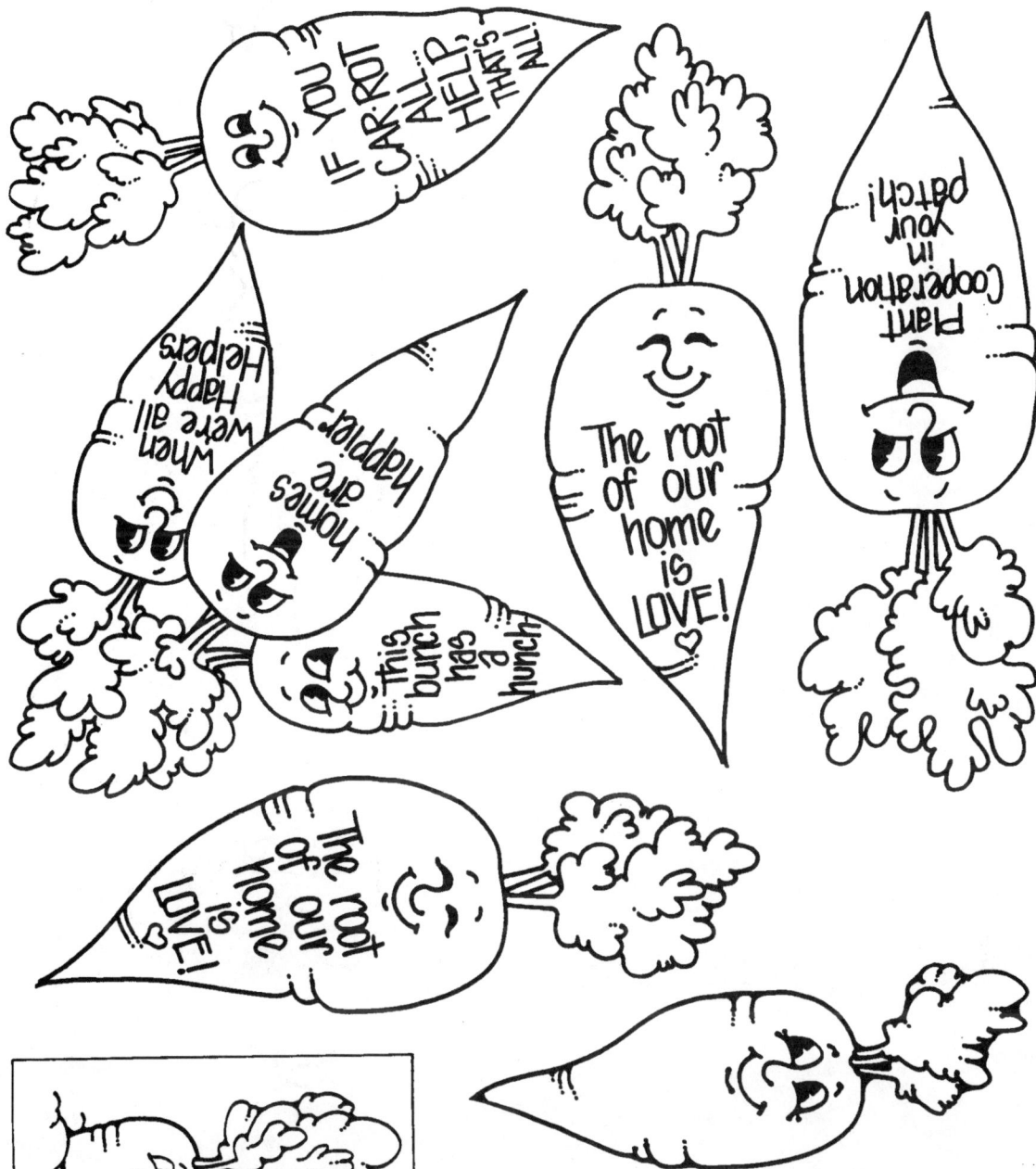

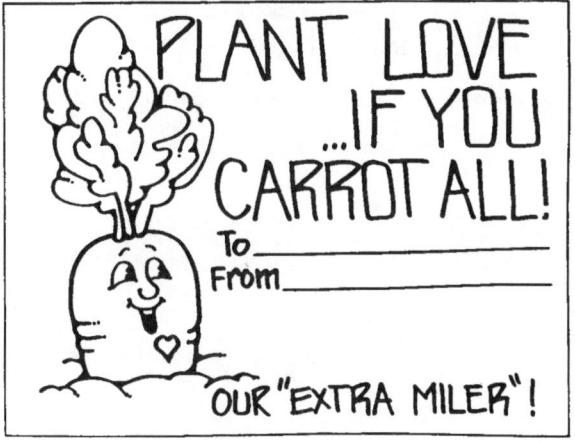

Pattern #4

The Do-Dots

Start with a half sheet of poster board. Next, brightly color all the little *Do-Dots* as well as the big *Do-Dot* title. Now, glue the title at the top of the poster board, turned sideways. Under the title, hinge the *Do-Dots* on the poster board in rows with clear tape at the top of each *Do-Dot*, and write under each *Do-Dot* the job that needs to be done. Each time a job is completed, your child should run back to the chart and lift up a new *Do-Dot* to see what to do next.

Use Symbols, Too

For young children who can't read, cut out the little job symbols included with the patterns and glue them under the *Do-Dots*. If tasks that you want your children to do are not illustrated by the job symbols or the ones you want do not fit, be *creative*. Draw simple illustrations or symbols yourself and tell the children what they stand for. Then they'll be off and *doing*.

After the above has been completed, use the illustrated *Do-Dots* working to decorate your chart or tape to the fridge as reminders of what *Do-Dots* do. Use the little badges and *Round of Applause* award to reinforce your children's good work habits. If you need more awards, you are authorized to duplicate enough for your children. Most important, have a lot of fun!

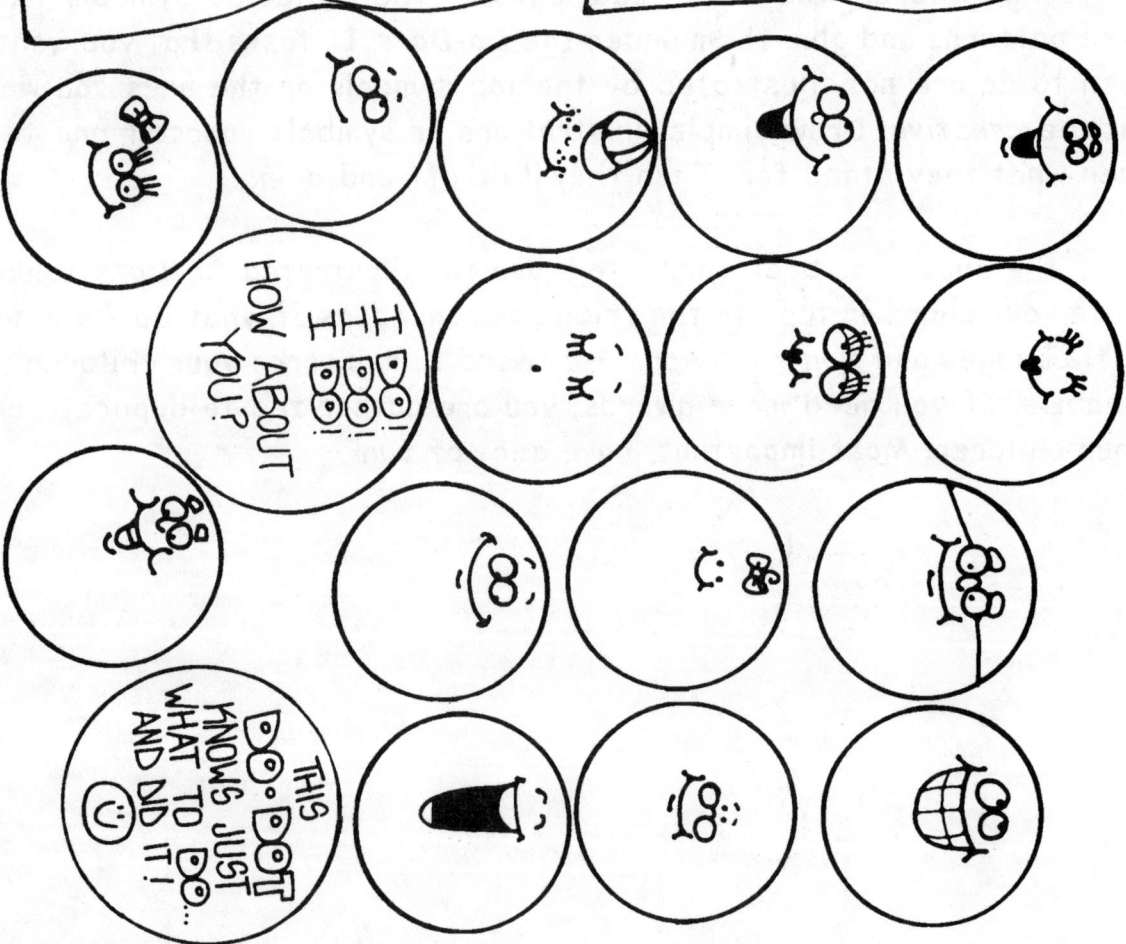

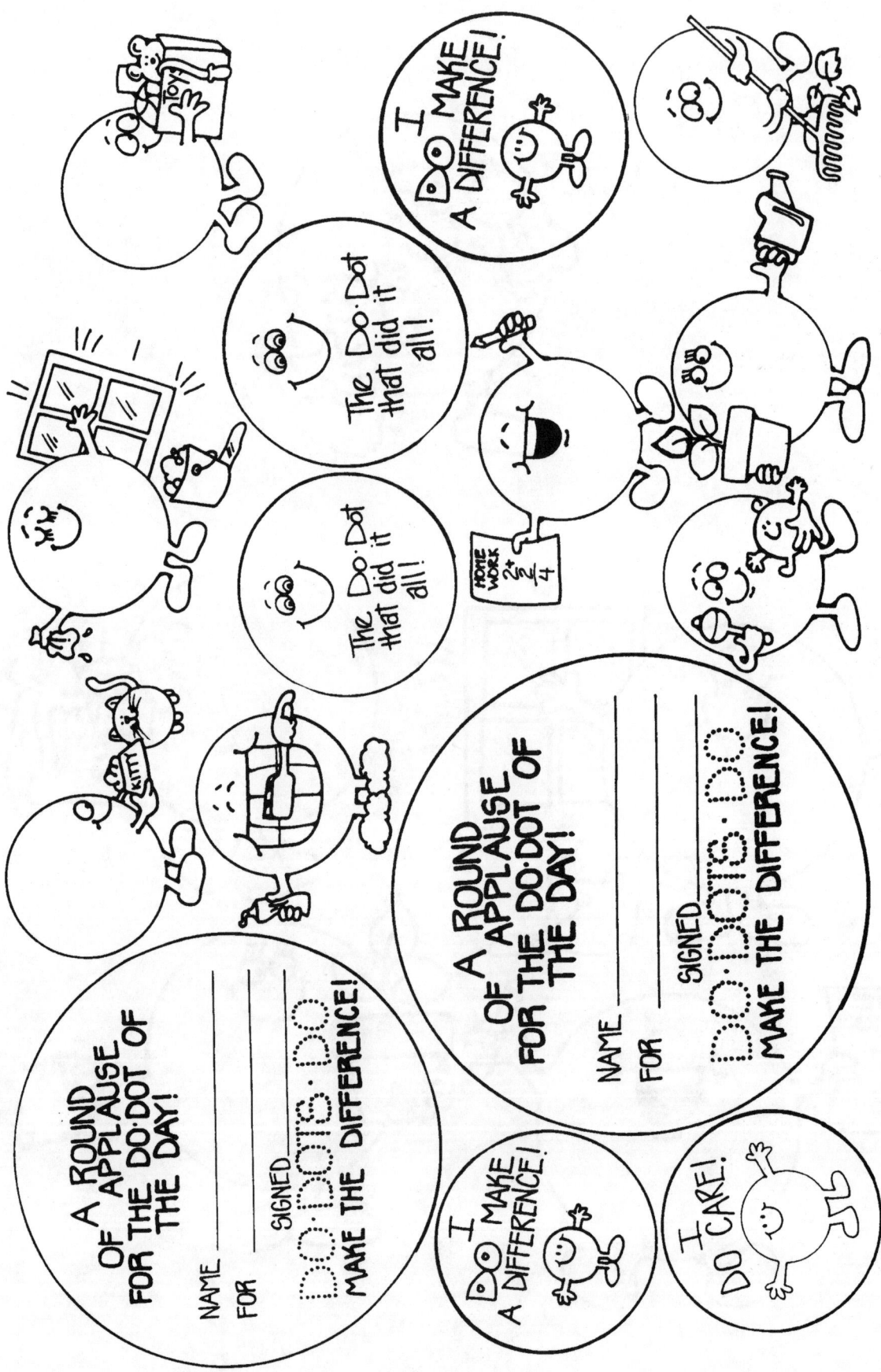

I DO MAKE A DIFFERENCE!

The Do·Dot that did it all!

The Do·Dot that did it all!

HOME WORK 2+ 2/4

A ROUND OF APPLAUSE FOR THE DO·DOT OF THE DAY!

NAME _____

FOR _____

SIGNED _____

DO·DOTS·DO MAKE THE DIFFERENCE!

A ROUND OF APPLAUSE FOR THE DO·DOT OF THE DAY!

NAME _____

FOR _____

SIGNED _____

DO·DOTS·DO MAKE THE DIFFERENCE!

I DO MAKE A DIFFERENCE!

I DO CAKE!

Pattern #5

Pizza Puzzle

If your family loves pizza, let your imagination go on this one. Introduce this job puzzle by having a pizza party. Make it special by bringing home the family's favorite take-out pizza, and get the excitement level up by decorating the table with a red-checked table cloth and candles.

Now color and cut out the pattern of the large pizza man and prominently display him along the lettering in the patterns, *I Met the Test and Did My Best*. Then, after the last yummy morsel of pizza is washed down with bubbly root beer, explain to the family that for the next little while, the *Mama Mia!* man (the pizza maker) is going to teach us how to meet the test by being our best at cooperating and doing our work. If we do, on _____ (date) we'll have another pizza party. During this period of time, use the two badges and the *Mama Mia!* award to keep the excitement going.

Using the Puzzle

Now the children are ready for the pizza (job) puzzle. First, write jobs by each number on the *numbered* pie pan and glue it to a piece of round poster board. Then color and cut out each individual piece of pizza. Put the numbered pie chart on the table in front of the children. They find job number one, which might be *make bed*. The children run and do that job, then come back to the table. They find the appropriate piece of pepperoni-numbered pizza that corresponds to the job they just did, and put the piece over the job. When the pizza is complete, they are done. Presto! Not only are the children doing work, but they're doing a puzzle and learning their numbers at the same time.

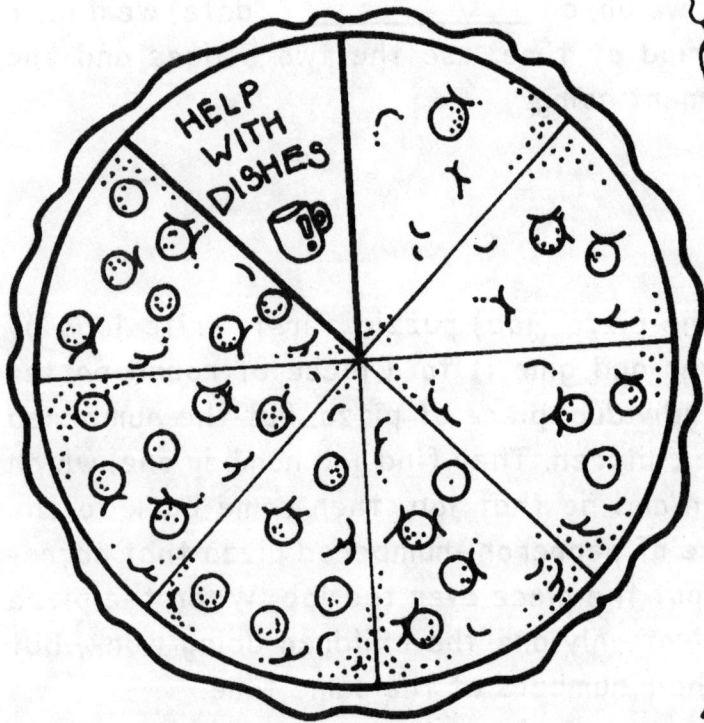

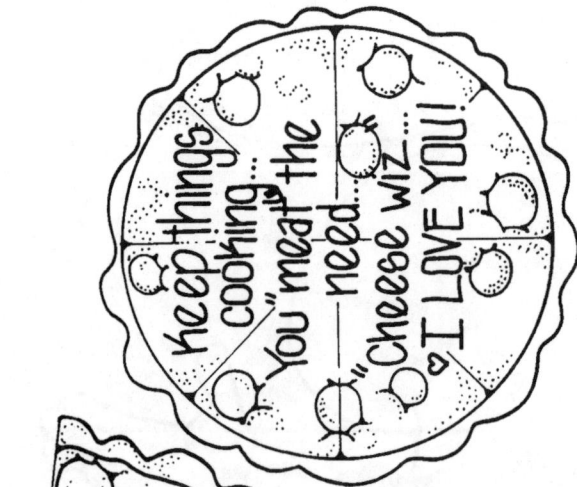

keep things
cooking...
"you "meat" the
need...
"cheese wiz...
♥I LOVE YOU!

to a
"peppi"
person
who
persisted!

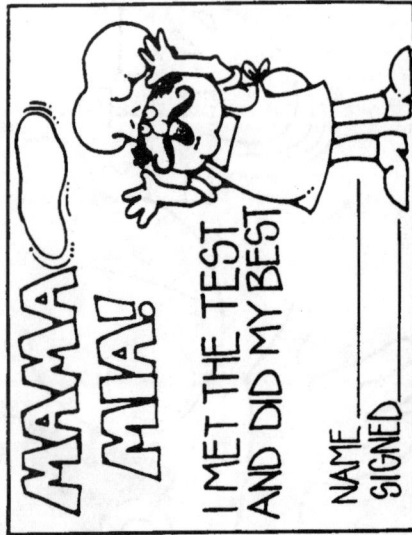

MAMA MIA!

I MET THE TEST
AND DID MY BEST

NAME _____
SIGNED _____

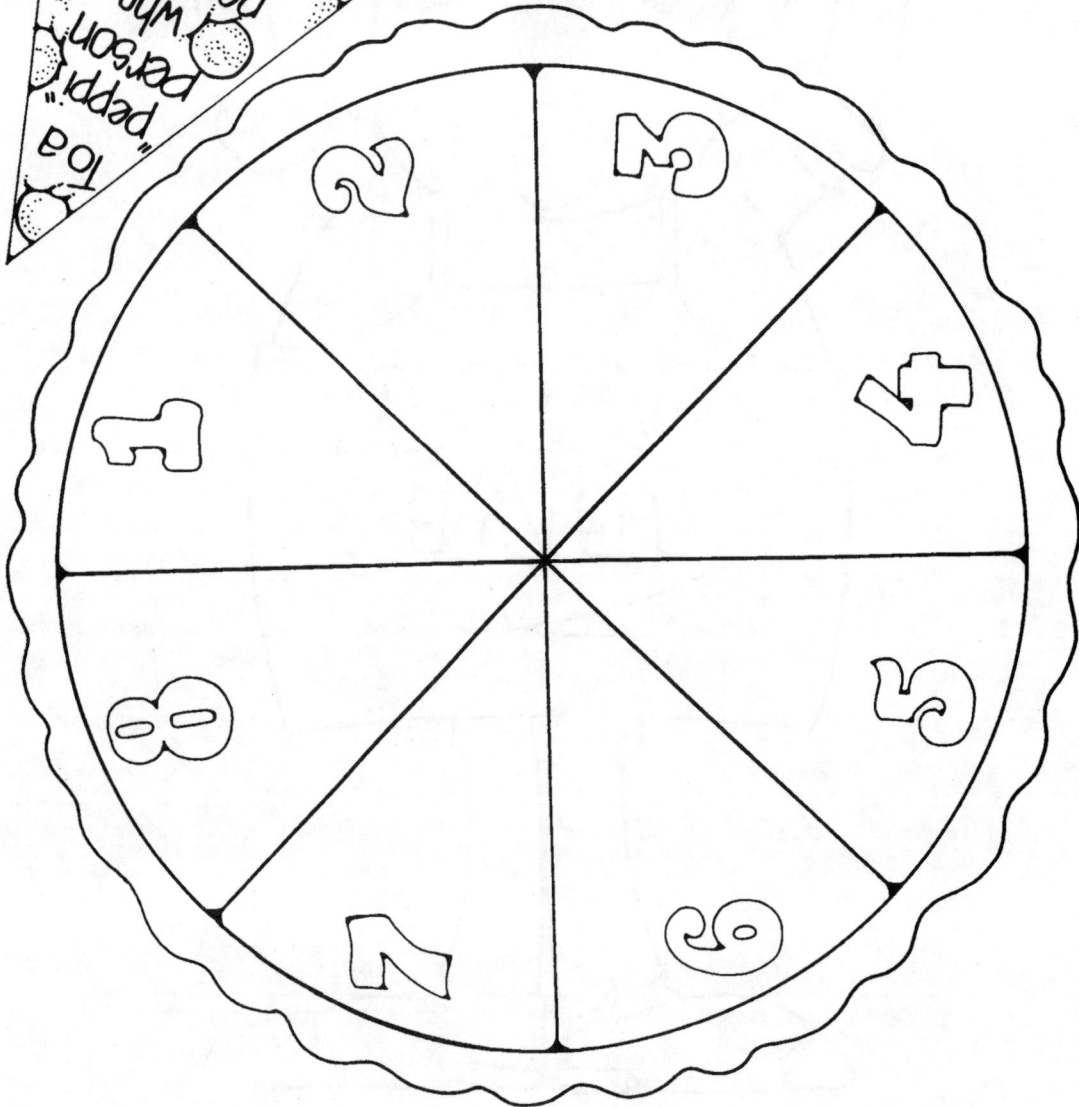

I met the test and did my best!

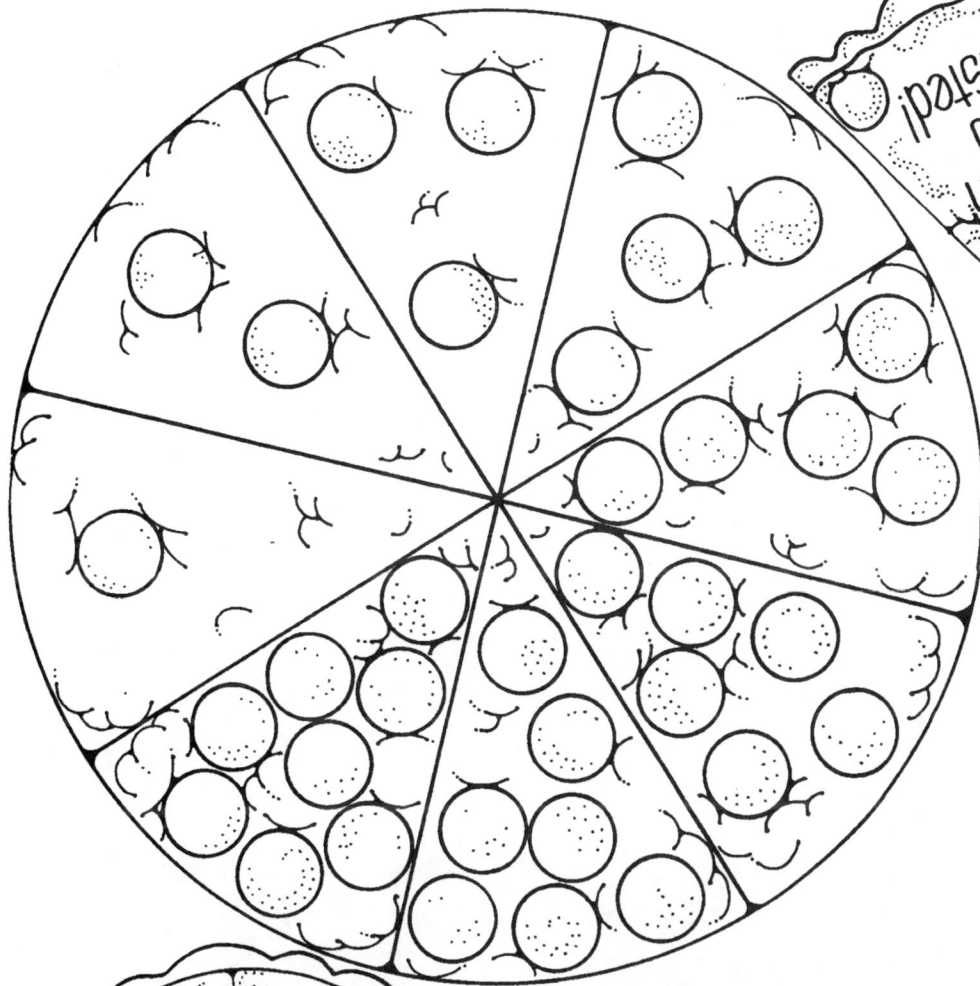

To a "peppi" person who persisted!

keep things cooking...
You "mea"t the need...
"Cheese wiz"...
I LOVE YOU!

MAMA MIA!

I MET THE TEST
AND DID MY BEST

NAME _____
SIGNED _____

Pattern #6

The Butterfly Chart

These patterns allow you to make two different charts. One we'll call *Job Butterflies* and the other *Flying High*, which has a special animation feature.

Job Butterflies

Start with the pattern with all the little butterflies on it. Color and then cut them out. Next, cover a half sheet of poster board with sky-blue construction paper. Glue on fluffed-up cotton balls for clouds. In between the clouds, hinge the butterflies with tape like you did the *Do-Dots,* so they can be lifted up to see the jobs written underneath.

I also devised a fun, complementary project to use with our butterfly chart. I found some tricot in the basement and cut out pieces in the shape of butterfly wings, sewed them together, and attached a loop of elastic to each side. This way the wings fit around the children's arms, and they flew merrily around the house like little butterflies while doing their work. My nine-year-old even got involved and enjoyed the whole process. (Moral: Don't count out older children.) This is a very simple concept, but very fun, especially for children with vivid imaginations. Before they know it, their work's all done!

Flying High

Use the large butterfly pattern for this one. On a large piece of poster board, write the child's jobs in big one-inch high letters down the left side. Title the chart using the child's name, such as *Betty Butterfly Flies High.* Then you *animate* your large butterfly, so it moves from the bottom of the chart higher and higher until all the jobs are done.

How do you animate? First, mount the large butterfly on poster board and cut it out. Cut holes in the top of the chart and the bottom, on the right side opposite the jobs. (See "Betty Butterfly Flies High" illustration.) Then run a string through each hole, making the string long enough to be tied in back. Make the knot small enough to fit through the holes at the top or the bottom, and also tie it loose enough so it can move easily when pulled. Attach the butterfly to the string by taping the string securely to the back of the poster board-reinforced butterfly. When a job is complete, move the butterfly up to the next job until it can't fly any higher. Then it's time for badges and an award.

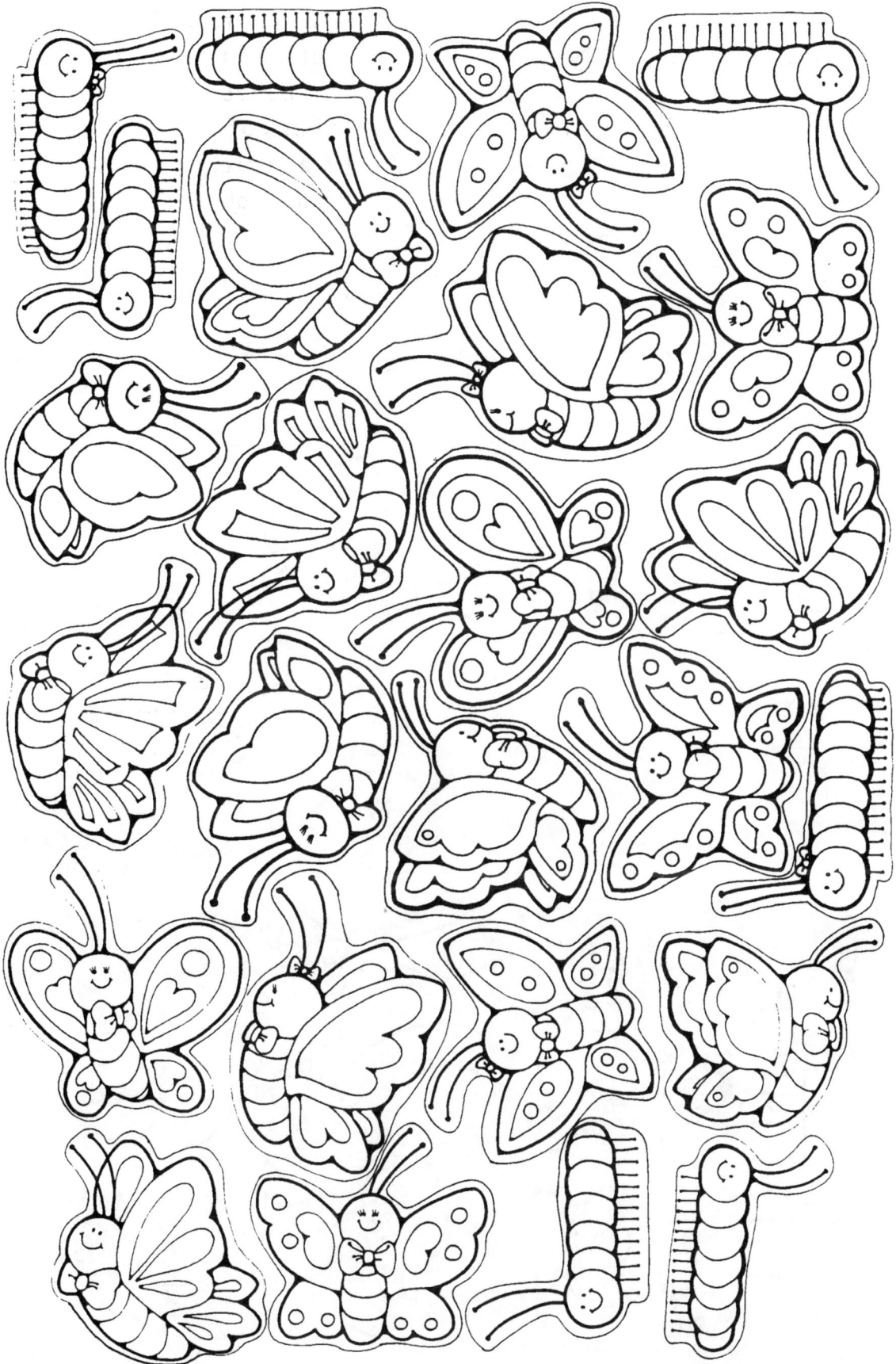

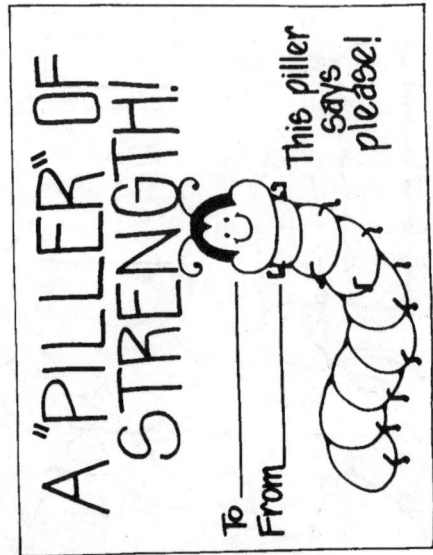

A "PILLER" OF STRENGTH!

To _____
From _____

This piller says please!

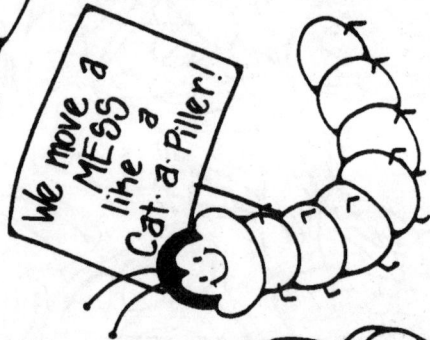

We move a MESS a like a Cat-a-Piller!

I'm a wing-ding doer!

I'm a wing-ding doer!

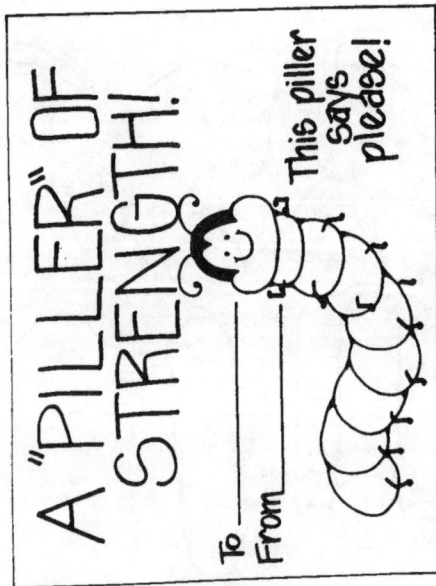

A "PILLER" OF STRENGTH!

To _____
From _____

This piller says please!

I'm a high flyin' helper!

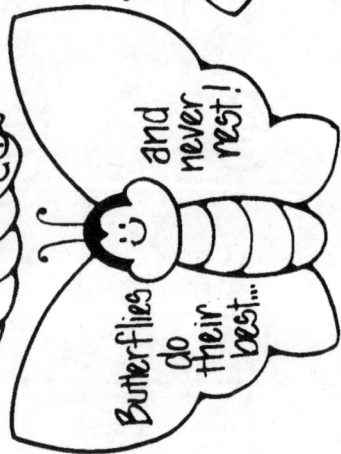

Butterflies do their best... and never rest!

32

Betty Butterfly Flies High

- Be happy
- Smile!
- Sweep Floor
- Empty Garbage
- Practice Piano
- Vacuum
- Brush teeth
- Set table
- Put toys away
- Get Dressed
- Comb Hair
- Make Bed

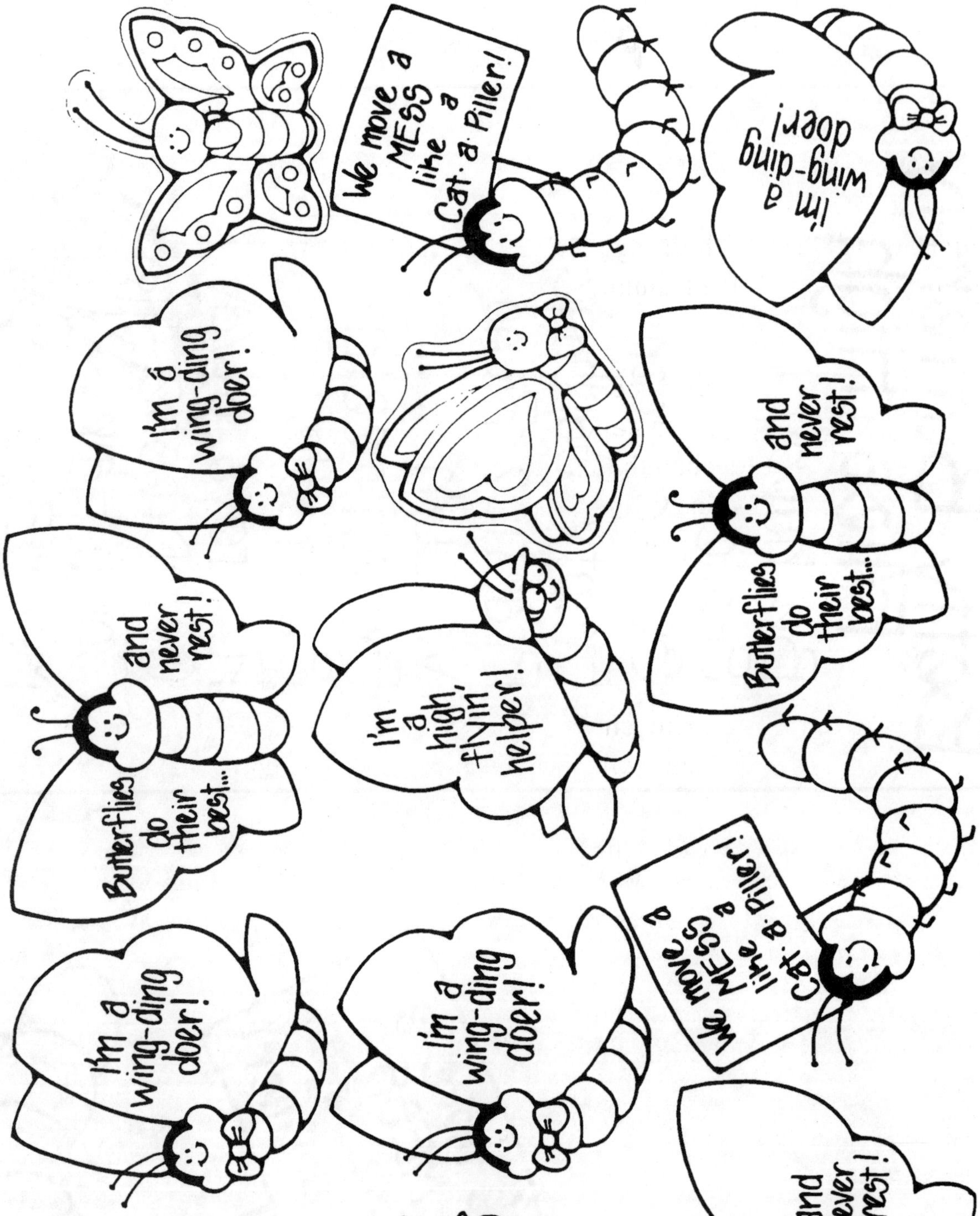

We move a
MESS a
like a
Cat-a-Piller!

I'm a
wing-ding
doer!

I'm a
wing-ding
doer!

and
never
rest!

and
never
rest!

I'm a
high,
flyin'
helper!

Butterflies
do
their
best...

Butterflies
do
their
best...

I'm a
wing-ding
doer!

I'm a
wing-ding
doer!

We move a
MESS a
like a
Cat-a-Piller!

and
never
rest!

I'm a
high,
flyin'
helper!

Butterflies
do
their
best...

Pattern #7

Ollie Octopus

Ollie's very handy at helping. So are the children who use this chart. There's not a big theme that goes along with Ollie. He's just for fun.

First, there's a large picture of Ollie doing a whole bunch of jobs—all at once. He's taking out the trash, sweeping the floor, dusting, doing dishes—even giving himself a bath, besides brushing his teeth. (Does an octopus have teeth? Oh, well, kids do.) Let the kids color Ollie the very best they know how and proudly display him where all can see.

Put Ollie Together

Now you're ready for the chart. You'll notice right away that Ollie is separated from his slithery tentacles; and the way we get him back together again is to do our jobs. Cut out each individual tentacle and write a job on the back of each one. Put Ollie's body on a piece of poster board, and when each job is done, one leg at a time, put Ollie back together again. It's so disconcerting to see Ollie all disjointed. (Use *Blue Tack* or other plastic clay adhesives to attach Ollie's legs—or good ol' thumbtacks on a piece of corkboard.)

Oh, yes, there are lots of badges that go with Ollie, like the *Handy Dandy Helper* badge or the *I've got to HAND it to YOU* badge and the award for *Often Offering Oceans of Optimistic O.K.'s When Asked To Lend Helping Hands*. Have fun with Ollie; that's what he's for—and a little cooperation, too!

I'M A HANDY HELPER!

MAKE BED PLEASE!

FOR OFTEN OFFERING OCEANS OF OPTIMISTIC "OK's" WHEN ASKED TO LEND HELPING HANDS!

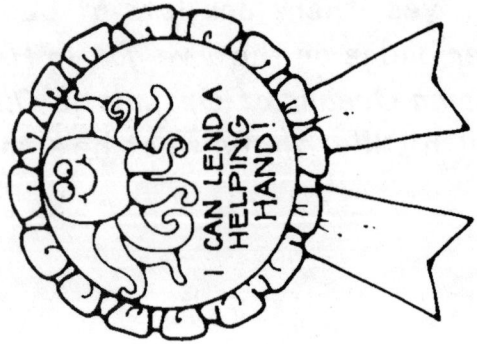

TO: _____

FROM: _____

I CAN LEND A HELPING HAND!

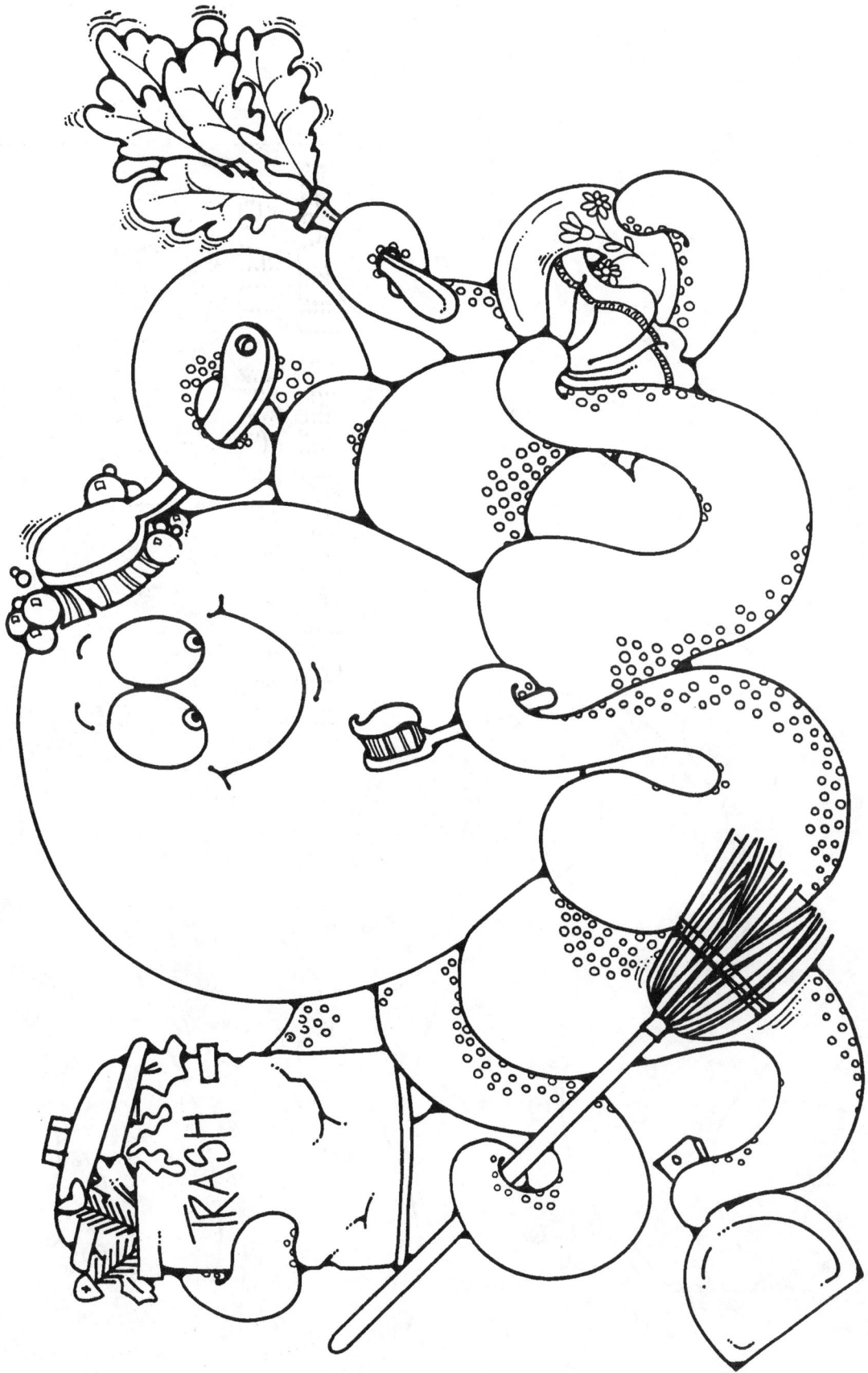

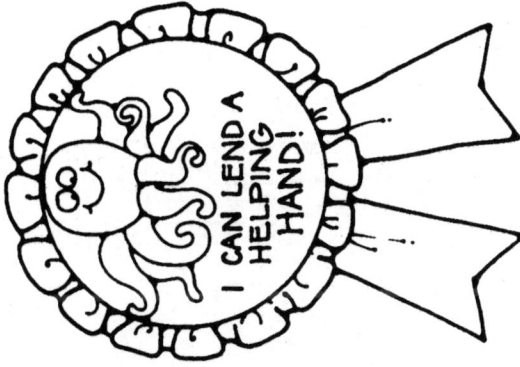

I CAN LEND A HELPING HAND!

OLLIE ALWAYS HELPS!

I've got to HAND it to YOU!

HANDY DANDY HELPER!

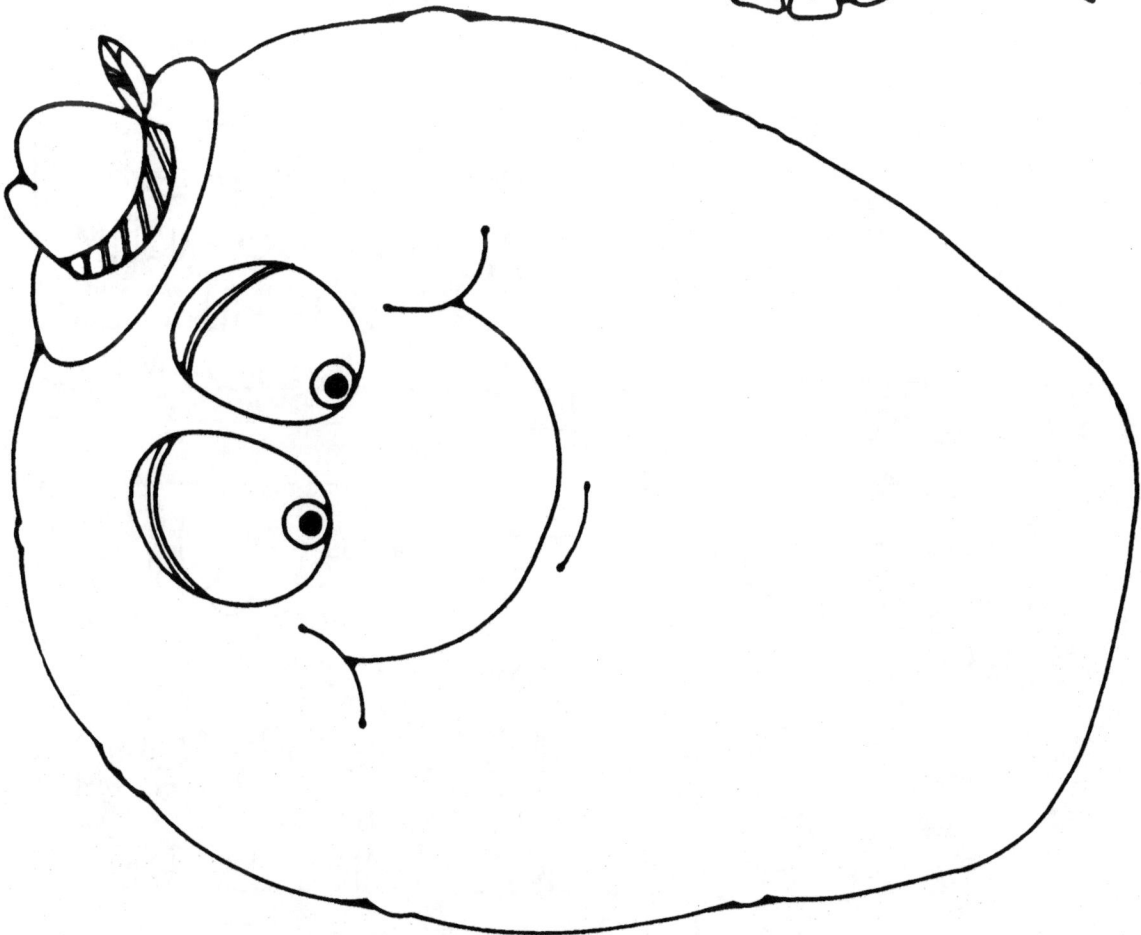

HANDY
DANDY
HELPER!

HANDY
HARRY
HELPER

I CAN LEND A
HELPING
HAND!

OLLIE
ALWAYS
HELPS!

I've got to to
HANDS it to
YOU!

FOR
OFTEN OFFERING OCEANS
OF OPTIMISTIC "O.K.'S"
WHEN ASKED TO LEND
HELPING HANDS!
TO:
FROM:

FOR
OFTEN OFFERING OCEANS
OF OPTIMISTIC "O.K.'S"
WHEN ASKED TO LEND
HELPING HANDS!
TO:
FROM:

FOR
OFTEN OFFERING OCEANS
OF OPTIMISTIC "O.K.'S"
WHEN ASKED TO LEND
HELPING HANDS!
TO:
FROM:

Pattern #8

I Never "Leaf" A Job Undone

We've given you lots of leaves to write your children's jobs on—enough so you won't have to *leaf* any job undone.

Start with the ample tree trunk, big enough to hold all your jobs. Put it on at least a half sheet of poster board, then color the leaves. *At this point you have two options.* First, you can write your jobs on the front of each leaf and stick it on the tree when the job is completed. (Stick it on with *Blue Tack* plastic clay adhesive, or mount the tree on a sheet of corkboard and use thumbtacks.) Or you can hinge each leaf to the tree with a strip of transparent tape and write a job underneath, so the child has to lift up the leaves to find out what jobs there are to do. Personally, I prefer putting on the leaves after the jobs are completed. It's fun to see the tree come to life as the work gets done.

More Than One Child Can Use This Chart

A suggestion when several kids are using the same tree: Color each child's leaves a different color. That way they can keep track, and it adds more color to the chart. Mom just needs to keep track of the leaves each day so they do not get misplaced.

These patterns have a set of badges with one unique feature. One large leaf badge is left blank so you may write your own little recognition statement—personalize it to your child's achievement. The award has a special treat for *stickin' to the job* by being entitled to a *stick of* gum.

Thanks for
stickin' with
it!
You never "LEAF" the job
undone!

Awarded to _____

This Award entitles you to a
"STICK" of GUM!

signed _____

Thanks for
stickin' with
it!
You never "LEAF" the job
undone!

Awarded to _____

This Award entitles you to a
"STICK" of GUM!

signed _____

♥Lily
♥Leaf♥
♥Love!

TO: _____
From: _____

I
turned
over
a
new leaf!
How about you?

I
turned
over
a
new leaf!
How about you?

A LOVE LEAF!
thanks for: _____

What a treat!

A LOVE LEAF!
thanks for: _____

"LEAF" IT
TO ME!
I GET THE
JOB DONE!

"LEAF" IT
TO ME!
I GET THE
JOB DONE!

Pattern #9

Going Fishing

This is more a game than a chart. It's also lots of fun and simple to do. First, color the little fish, cut them out, and write the jobs you want your children to do on the back. Then attach paper clips to the front part of each fish.

Next, tie a magnet on the end of a string, with the other end tied to a *fishing pole*. Put all the little fish in a big glass bowl or spread them out on a plate. Then the kids go *fishing*. Out comes a little fish, then they go do the job written on the back. Repeat this delightful process over and over until the jobs are all done.

If Mom wants the kids to do the jobs in order, the kids can go fishing in front of a little screen, and Mom can put selected jobs on the magnet.

Top off this fun little project with the badges and the special award that shows off the kids who are *hooked on helping*.

Help With Dishes

I'm fishing with fantastic bait, for someone who will help till late!

I'm fishing with fantastic bait, for someone who will help till late!

FANCY FISH full of HELPFULNESS!

HALIBUT HELPER!

the star fish!

Sea-horsens not for me... I'm as helpful as can be!

I'm never crabby, when I help out!

the star fish!

I'm fishing with fantastic bait, for someone who will help till late!

Sea-horsens not for me... I'm as helpful as can be!

NAME THAT TUNA!
Sorry Charlie!
It may sound fishy but... I'm hooked on helping!
name _____
signed _____

NAME THAT TUNA!
Sorry Charlie!
It may sound fishy but... I'm hooked on helping!
name _____
signed _____

50

Pattern #10

I Give A Hoot

This is another theme/game job chart. It places a great deal of emphasis on caring by teaching the children to *Give A Hoot*. There are four elements to this chart/game:

1. **The little pictures of the owls.** These show up all over the house to serve as reminders to *Give A Hoot*. Put them on the inside of the back door, on the fridge, on kitchen windows, bathroom mirrors, bedroom doors, closet doors, etc.

2. **The BIG picture of the owl.** This will *be* colored and put in a central place where all your job charts are kept. Cut out the lettering, *Give A Hoot,* and tape it above or below the big owl.

3. **The Give A Hoot Game.** This is a board game and job chart all in one. Cut out the illustration of the game, color it, and mount it on a piece of poster board. Here's how you play: Start with a playing piece for every child. This can be something as simple as a button, or borrow regular playing pieces from the family game closet.

Each morning, or whenever you do your household work as a family, start the game over. All players begin on the square labeled *Start*. Everyone moves ahead to the first task. When the job indicated on the square is completed, the child can move his playing piece to the next square and start on that responsibility. But before he does, he has to give a *toot* on a party horn *for giving a hoot*. **NOTE:** All jobs listed on the game will *not be* appropriate for certain children. Mom or Dad are the only ones with authority to say that the child may skip that particular job and go on to the next.

4. **Incentives.** *There* are several incentives besides playing a game that will motivate children to get their jobs done. Of course, the *badges and award* included in the patterns are the place to start. But there are other fun things for *handy hoots who help.*

Put the children on a point system by awarding a certain number of *heart stickers* when they get their jobs done. These stickers can be placed by each child's name on a piece of poster board. Stickers like these may be found at novelty, craft, or gift stores. Encourage the children by giving stickers even when they try. Just watch; they'll do even better next time.

Hand out rewards when the children get a certain number of stickers. For example, ten *give a hoot* stickers could earn a new pair of barrettes, or 15 could earn a special toy or a new pair of socks. List all the things the kids could receive, and next to them on the same sheet of paper write the point total they have to achieve in order to receive the item. This will be lots of fun while it enhances cooperation in your home.

OURS
IS A
NEAT
NEST

HOOT

Birds of
a feather
work
together!

Happy Hoots
help
at home!

HANDY, HELPFUL,
HOOTS
MAKE ME HAPPY!

Be wise
you guys,
don't criticize...
so lets not hear
a peep, until you've
gone to sleep!

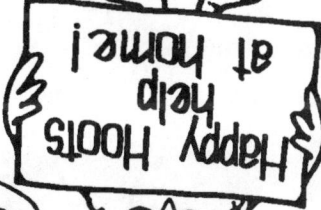

HIP HIP HOO-RAY!
Here's a
Hoot Hero
who helped!
awarded to ____
for wise conduct
signed ____
Admiral Bird

HIP HIP HOO-RAY!
Here's a
Hoot Hero
who helped!
awarded to ____
for wise conduct
signed ____
Admiral Bird

GIVE

I LOVE YOU

54

HOOTS HOLD THEIR TEMPERS...
EVEN WHEN IT'S HARD!
If YOU have, go ahead one space!

Think of something very wise to do around your bird house!

HIP HIP HOOT-RAY!
I'm here to stay!
DONE AT LAST!
Give one loud HOOT and TOOT

HOOTS HELP! WITH DISHES!
give a HOOT then give a TOOT!

GIVE A HOOT!
HELP WITHOUT BEING ASKED!

HAPPY HOOT'S ARE HAPPY HELPERS

HOME ♡ TWEET ♡ HOME

EMPTY GARBAGE WHEN NEEDED...
then move ahead Please!

VACUUM ONE TREE or ROOM

REMEMBER NOT TO "PECK" ON OTHERS

BE WISE! CHECK UNDER BED FOR TOYS

who's who
when you're wise and use your eyes, you will find a pleasant suprise!!!

GIVE A HOOT AND TOOT

FLY AND PICK UP TOYS

Give a hoot then give a toot!

EAT EVERYTHING AND CLEAN UP... GIVE A HOOT!
GIVE A TOOT!

BRUSH YOUR BEAK!
And give a HOOT after every meal!

BIRDS OF A FEATHER ARE KIND WHEN TOGETHER!
say one nice word then give a HOOT, and TOOT!!!

OR TAKE A BIRD BATH! give a HOOT!

WASH FACE

who
will be the first HOOT home?

COMB HAIR or FEATHERS
give a HOOT!

GET DRESSED
and give a HOOT!

MAKE A BED
give a HOOT!

START

55

Pattern #11

Minute Minder

Time is important. We've all heard the phrase, *time is money*. But also important is the *peace of mind* that comes from *time well spent*. That usually means we've used our time to accomplish something that we really wanted to do. Sometimes, however, there are things that *must* be done before we can do what we want to do. That's how it is with tasks around the house. Therefore, we want to get housework done quickly. And if all in our home cooperate, *everyone* can do the things they want to do, *sooner*.

The theme of this job chart is *Minute Minder*. It's basically to see *how fast we can get the job done right*. However, let me underscore a very important point. You may be tempted to introduce competition with this theme. My recommendation is *not* to see who can be *the first one done*, or *who* can *do their work the fastest*, because every time we create a winner, we also create a loser. The object of *Minute Minder* is to help our children not waste their time and to quickly do their work so they can do other things.

Time Jobs

To create this chart, cut out the two parts of the timer, color them, mount them each on a piece of poster board, and write the jobs on the pie sections of the timer. Then attach the round face of the timer with the cut-out slot matching exactly with the pie sections to reveal each job. Attach the face to the timer through the center with a metal brad (the flexible metal prongs bend along the back of the chart to keep it together). When the face rotates, the children see one job at a time.

Use the award and little badges as reminders of how important time is. As the children do their work, put on fun, *fast* music that will get them moving. (Try a marching band.) As they finish their work, tell the children exactly how many minutes it took them to do it. Write down each child's time, and encourage them to see if they can beat their time tomorrow. This fosters self-improvement rather than competition and teaches them to mind their minutes.

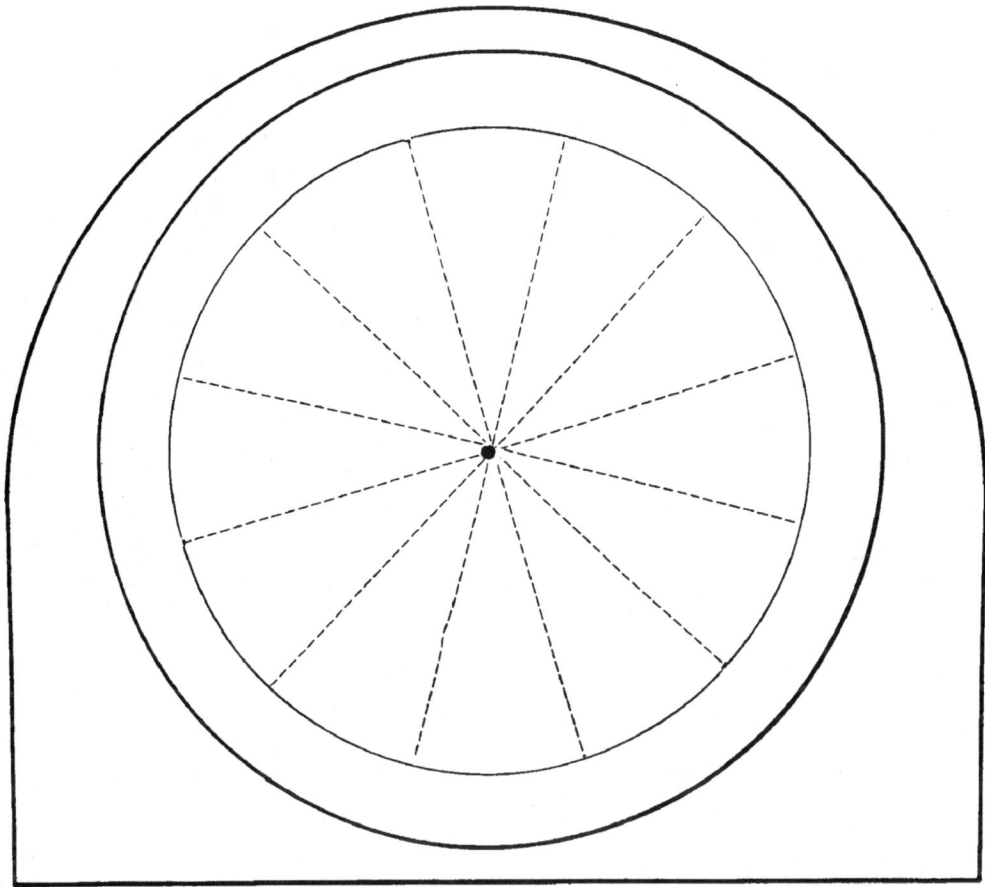

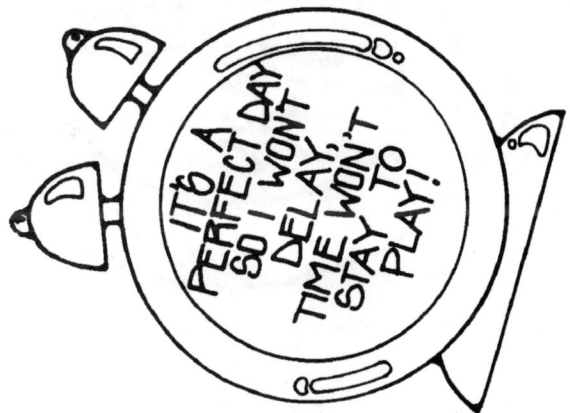

It's a perfect day, so I won't delay. Time won't stay, to play!

Do your best today, without delay. And it will pay, to live the right way!

I'm Mighty Minute Minder...
When time starts to fly—I fly faster!
name_____
signed_____

I'm a winner! not a whiner!
JUST A REMINDER

"FACE" the FACTS WHEN TO DO YOUR TASKS!

"FACE" the FACTS WHEN TO DO YOUR TASKS!

I TICK·TICK CLICK·CLICK NEVER, NEVER, NEVER QUIT!

IT'S A PERFECT DAY SO I WON'T DELAY, TIME WON'T STAY TO PLAY!

I'm Mighty Minute Minder...
When time starts to fly—I fly faster!
name_____
signed_____

DO YOUR BEST TODAY, WITHOUT DELAY-AND IT WILL PAY TO LIVE THE RIGHT WAY!

I TICK·TICK CLICK·CLICK NEVER, NEVER, NEVER QUIT!

61

Pattern #12

Cooperative Clown

The job chart for *Cooperative Clown* can work in two ways. After you've colored and cut out the big clown, mount him on a full sheet of poster board. Now you have two options for using the *job balloons:*

1. Color the balloons different bright colors and place them in a bunch on the poster board, drawing strings to the hand of the clown as if they were helium-filled and the clown was holding them. Then attach the balloons by hinging them at the top with clear tape so the children may lift them up to see their jobs written underneath.

2. The second option is to write the jobs on the fronts of the balloons. Then place all the balloons on the kitchen counter or in the same room where you have *Cooperative Clown.* When the children complete each job, they can then put the balloons around the clown by using a plastic clay adhesive. This adhesive is readily available, is non-toxic, and is great for holding up posters, party decorations, trim, pictures, etc.

Bring the Circus Home

You'll want to create a circus atmosphere that the kids will really respond to before you introduce this chart. Start with a party; call it *The Greatest Home on Earth Party.* Decorate the kitchen with crepe paper. Go to the library and find some circus music you can play; also check out circus story books for added fun. Make signs out of poster board and put them around the house. They might read: *I can help without a frown, even though I'm not a Clown. Be "I Can" Clowns.*

With dinner you may want to have a clown salad, and for dessert, Clown Ice Cream Cones.

Clown Salad

To create the clown salad, start with a half peach for the head. Then add a cherry for the nose and mouth, raisins for the eyes, and cottage cheese for the hair. Use a slice of pear for a hat and place all of this on a bed of lettuce. They'll eat every bit.

Clown Ice Cream Cones

Scoop the ice cream into several nice round balls ahead of time and freeze it hard. Use a sugar cone for the hat, raisins for the eyes, cherry for the nose and mouth, and whipped cream stiffened with coconut for the hair. Serve these and watch the delight.

After dinner, have everybody sit in a circle, and you act as ringmaster. Introduce the chart, and as you tell about everyone's jobs, give it a little fanfare. For example: "Ladies and Gentleman, introducing the One and Only Daring Dishwasher (your child's name). May I draw your attention to the bathtub ring. Whoops! It's all gone because of our World Famous Bathtub Cleaner (your child's name)." Use lots of adjectives when describing your kids, such as: The Amazing, The Most Spectacular, The Very Special, The Outstanding, and on and on.

Have fun with *Cooperative Clown* and all the charts in this book. Remember to be sure and praise the children generously when they complete their tasks. That's why I've provided the badges and awards to help you in this important process. Recognizing your children's accomplishments is essential to creating an *atmosphere* of and *desire for* cooperation in your home. *May you have success!*

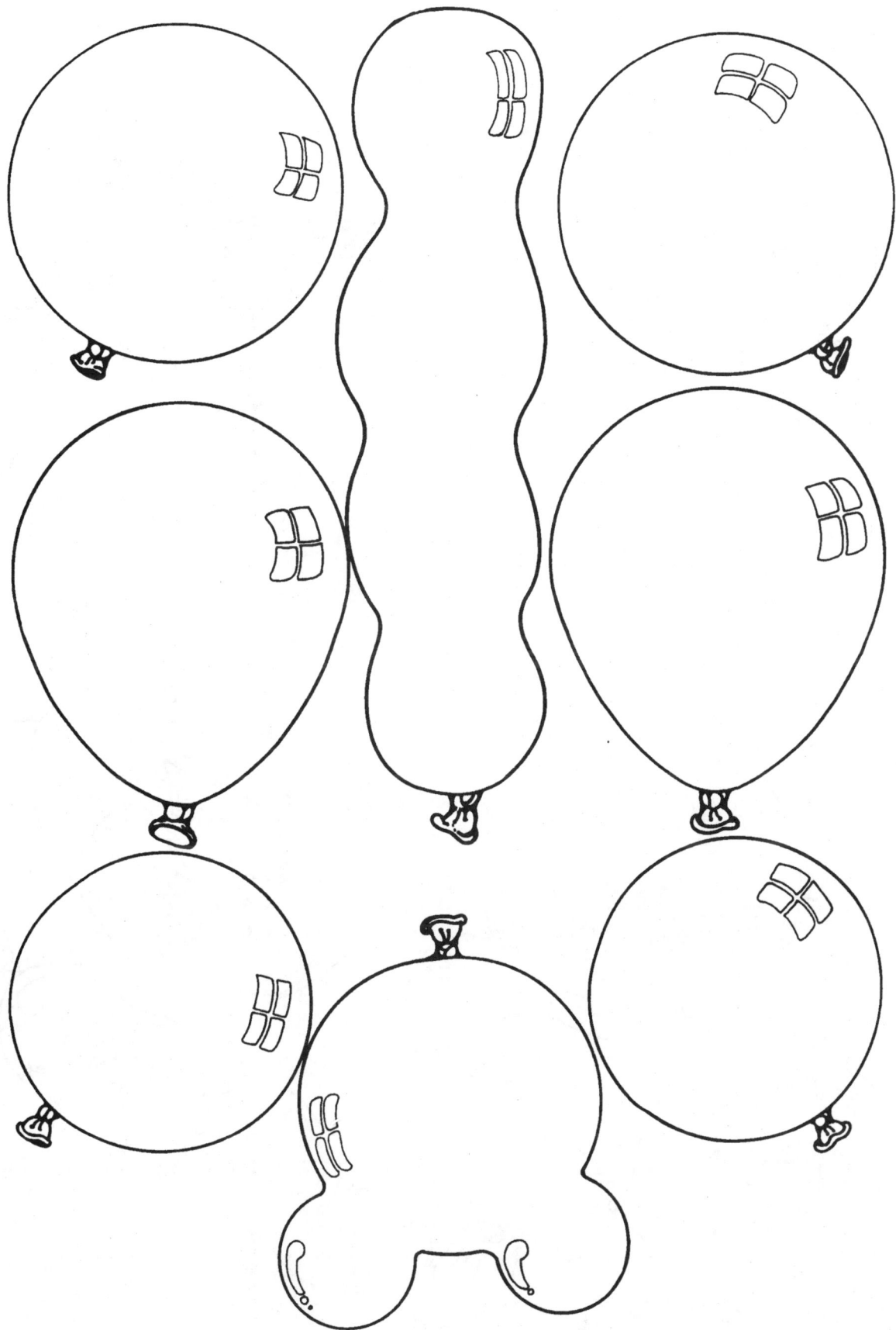

I'm the happiest
clown in town...
I never work
with a frown!
Awarded to_____
signed_____

I'm the happiest
clown in town...
I never work
with a frown!
Awarded to:_____
Signed:_____

I'm the happiest
clown in town...
I never work
with a frown!
Awarded to_____
Signed_____

I'm the happiest
clown in town...
I never work
with a frown!
Awarded to:_____
Signed:_____

Crazy
Clowns can
Clean Closets,
Carpets, cans, and
all sorts of things—
They can!
They can!

I can help
even though
I'm not
without a frown!
CLOWN!

I CAN CLOWN!

CORNY CLOWN CAN CLEAN!

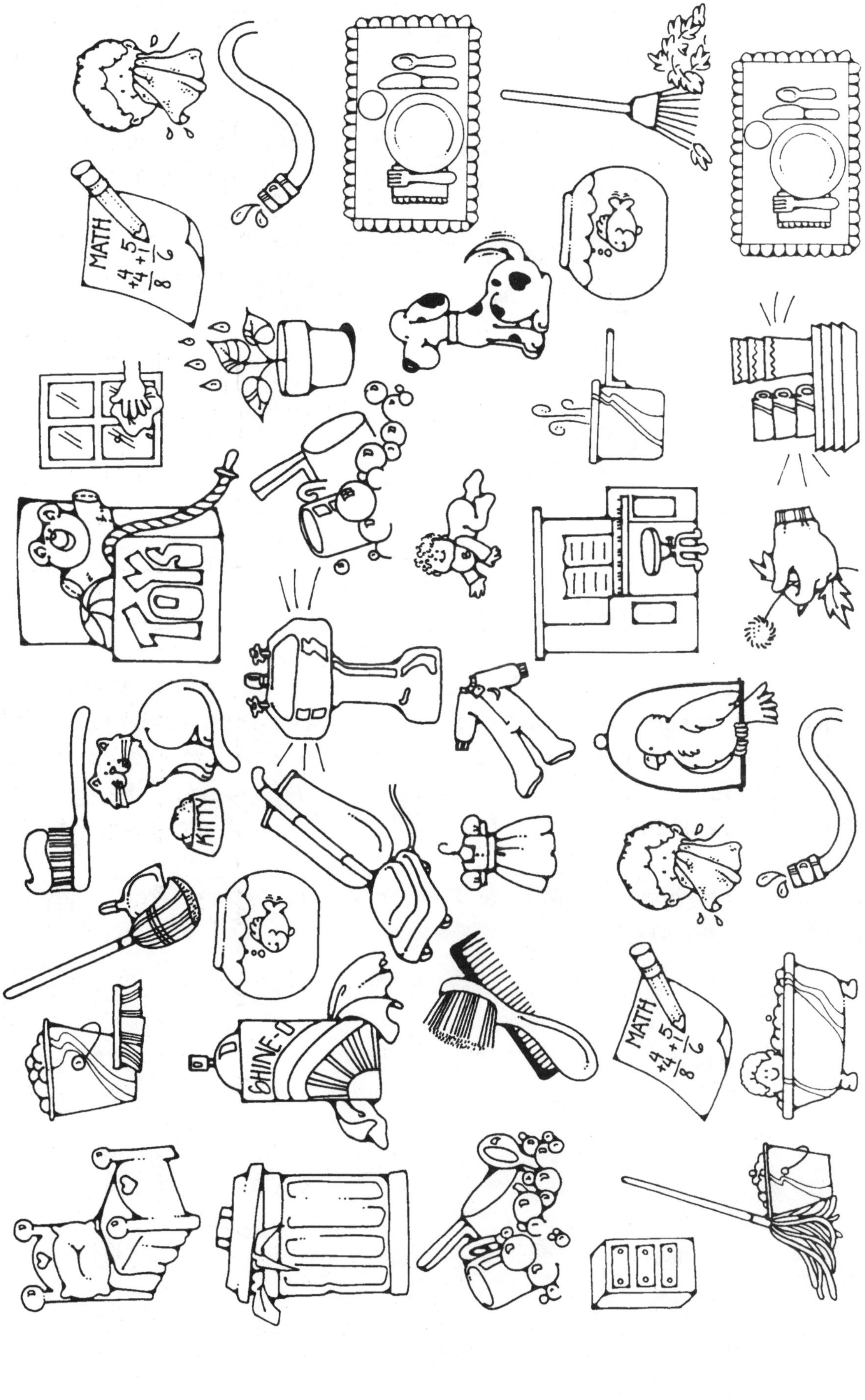
MATH
TOYS
KITTY
SHINE-O
MATH

About the Author

Suzanne Hansen is a popular writer and lecturer who specializes in helping parents discover the elements of fun and cooperation in family life. She has been called a modern-day Mary Poppins, and her books and presentations are brimming with hundreds of unique and original ideas that motivate children to help in happy ways. A master of positive teaching, she has shared the podium with Art Linkletter and many other leading parenting experts. She is also a popular Education Week speaker, and has co-directed and been a speaker at many EFY programs

Suzanne and her husband, Michael, live in West Jordan, Utah. They are the parents of three children.